OCTOBER 20 – DECEMBER 2 2006

# JOHN KEANE
## GUANTANAMERICA

John Keane's terrifying images of Guantanamo Bay evoke the actual horror of Guantanamo Bay with an acute imaginative understanding that only a true artist can provide. Guantanamo Bay is a concentration camp run by the "leader of the free world", the bastion of "civilised society" in its battle against "evil". The evil of course is embodied in this scandalous and obscene structure, created by the United States with the despicable complicity of this country.

This is a brilliant, important and properly appalling exhibition.

**Harold Pinter, London**

## Guantanamo: A Primer

John Keane's journey from Official Artist during the first Gulf War to Guantanamo Bay continues his tradition of looking at images that the rest of us would rather not see. The work in this exhibit must be set in context, for Guantanamo has become a metaphor for a range of recent policies adopted by the Bush Administration in the wake of the horrible attacks of September 11, 2001. As the lead lawyer challenging the Bush Administration's Guantanamo trial policy, I have been enmeshed in these issues for the past four years. And so I am delighted to accept the kind invitation from one of my favorite galleries worldwide, Flowers, to provide some context for Keane's work.

The Guantanamo Naval Base is in the territory of the Republic of Cuba. The United States occupies the base under a 1903 Lease Agreement with Cuba, which was extended by a 1934 Treaty. Under the terms of that lease, the United States has "complete jurisdiction and control," while Cuba retains "ultimate sovereignty." One of the more interesting aspects of this lease is that in order for it to be altered, *both* parties must agree (a lease arrangement I am sure most New Yorkers would love to have). So the rent for this part of the island, an enclave larger than Manhattan, remains $4085 per year. (Cuba indignantly refuses to cash America's checks for this paltry amount.) The base operates its own schools, power system, water supply, and internal transportation system.

The Administration has brought over 700 detainees captured from around the world to Guantanamo. The detainees hail from dozens of nations. While President Bush has claimed that the 450 men who reside there are all dangerous terrorists, no substantiation for that claim has been made (and some published reports contradict it). Because of the veil of secrecy surrounding Guantanamo, it is impossible to know who is right.

The Administration could have brought the detainees to the United States, or military bases around the world, but it chose Guantanamo. It did so not because it favored the weather there, but because of a rather dubious legal theory. The theory was that Cuba owned Guantanamo, and so the protections of the United States Constitution could not protect individuals there – even when the individuals were being detained by the United States. In essence, according to the Administration, Guantanamo was a legal black hole where it could do whatever it wanted – including torture the individuals – and face no legal consequences whatsoever. The results were sadly predictable.

And the legal claims in support of this black hole were none too convincing. The President claimed that Cuba had sovereignty over Guantanamo, despite the facts that the United States has this indefinite lease on the island and that it refuses to permit Cuban law to apply to the detainees. I have traveled to Guantanamo several times. It looks and feels like America. The signs are in English. McDonalds and Starbucks are there. And from top-to-bottom you feel no other source of law and order than that from America.

The President took the further remarkable step of attempting, on his own, to create a military trial system at Guantanamo to try some of these detainees. These military tribunals looked nothing like American trials – either civilian trials or courts-martial. Rather, they deprived defendants of the most basic rights, including the right to hear the evidence against them. The tribunals blatantly violated the most foundational international treaties ratified by the United States, such as the Geneva Conventions. All the while, they were designed to dispense the most awesome powers of government—including the death penalty. And they were set up without any involvement by Congress at all.

In March of this year, I argued a case in the United States Supreme Court, *Hamdan v. Rumsfeld*, that challenged this policy on behalf of Salim Hamdan, an alleged driver to Usama Bln Laden. I was supported by dozens of organizations around the world, including Retired Generals and Admirals of the United States military, former Secretary of State Albright, and prominent conservative scholars, who filed over 40 friend-of-the-court briefs. Most relevant for Keane's work was the fact that over 400 members of the United Kingdom and European Parliaments formally took a position in the case, claiming the Guantanamo policy violated international law. Their brief to the Court was signed by the leaders of all of the major political parties in Britain, including the Conservative Party.

On June 29, 2006, the Supreme Court sided with Mr. Hamdan. It found that President Bush's tribunals both lacked the basic fairness of American military law and violated the Geneva Conventions. Just think of it: a man with a fourth-grade Yemeni education accused of conspiring with one of the world's most evil men sued the President in the nation's highest court – and won. America is strong enough to permit such a challenge, and fair enough to let that challenge proceed. And America is wise enough to let such a decision stand as the law of the land – and to celebrate it as a vindication of the Rule of Law. For on that day, Hamdan won something that every American has celebrated from the Declaration of Independence on – a fair trial.

What makes America great is not the quality of the soil on which we stand, but the principles that define our nation. My parents came here from a distant land, attracted by that promise, of inalienable rights for all and equal opportunity. We are a land of justice and fairness, and with a system that is strong enough to handle even the most extraordinary of challenges. And so let us all hope that the wonderful work of Mr. Keane will be shortly seen as an archive of a dark day in American history that is not to return.

**Neal Katyal** is a law professor at Georgetown University Law Center. He previously served as National Security Adviser at the United States Department of Justice, law clerk to Justice Steven Breyer of the United States Supreme Court, and as a Visiting Professor at Harvard and Yale Law Schools.

The series entitled Guantanamerica grew from downloaded low resolution internet images of the Camp X - Ray detainees of Guantanamo Bay. I began to explore the dehumanising process in a digital manner on the computer as an analogy of the essential dehumanisation of the internment itself. From these manipulated images the paintings emerged.

The ambiguity of the submissive postures of the detainees interested me - were they attitudes of submissive obedience to their captors, or could they be attitudes of prayer (Islam meaning 'submission')? The low resolution of the images enhanced this ambiguity.

Further explorations on the computer began to reveal patterns not dissimilar to the kind of light interference effects observed when an oil film is dispersed on water.

Another analogy suggested itself: we can draw a direct line of consequence between the political and military interference necessitated in the pursuit of diminishing oil reserves and the enmity generated in extreme Islamic belief (Islamic countries having the greatest oil fields in the world).

The phenomenon of the Guantanamo detainees, iconic in their fluorescent orange suits, succeeds in being counterproductive rather than counter-terrorist. As is so often the case, efforts to suppress the symptoms of terrorism provide ample propaganda to fan the flames they seek to put out. It takes a leap of imagination to address the causes of disease, not just fight the symptoms. Sadly for the world, we see plenty of 'intelligence', but not much imagination.

**John Keane**

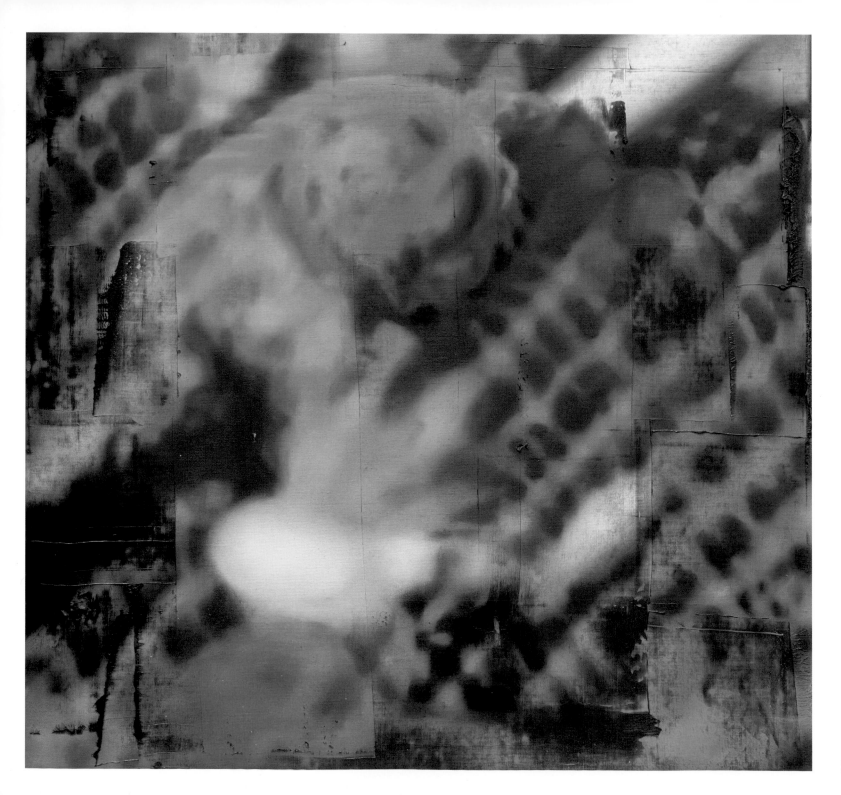

3

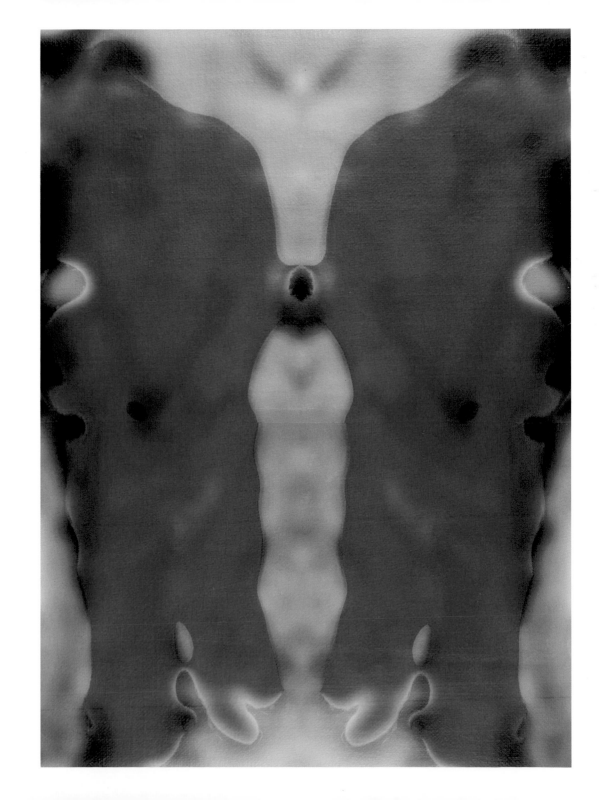

12

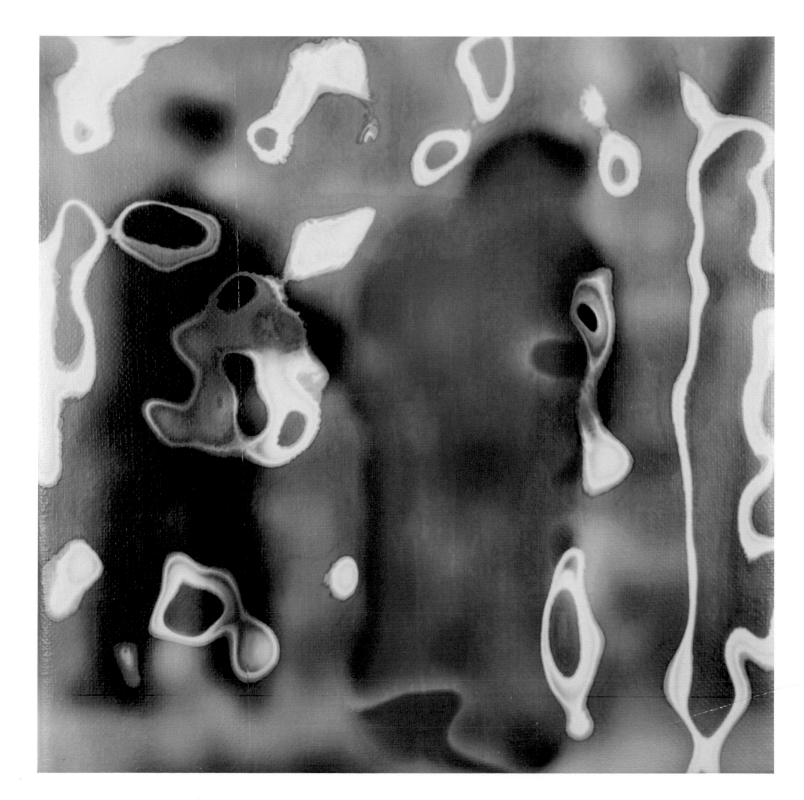

14

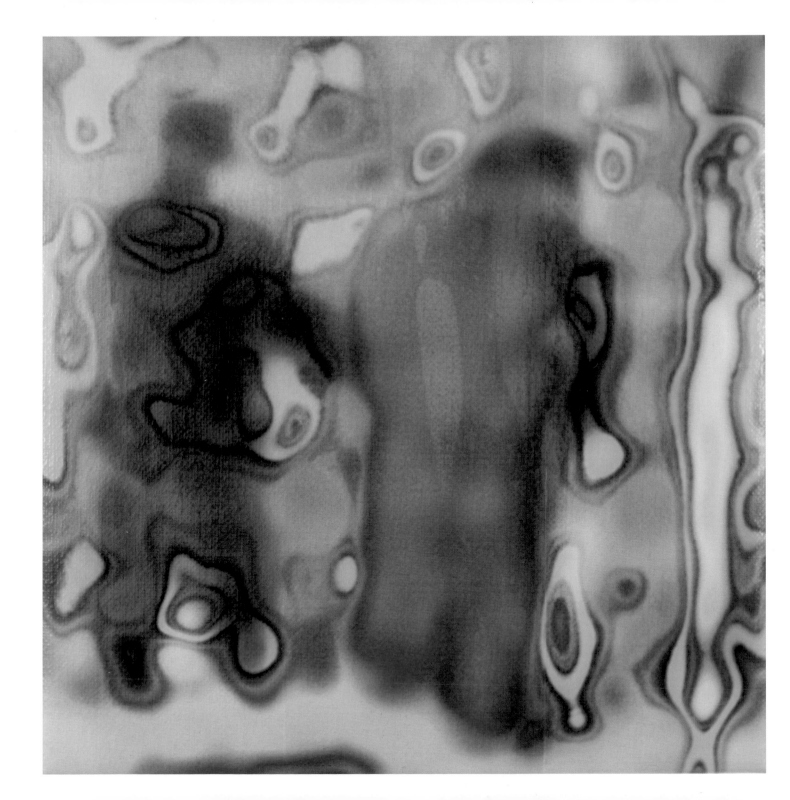

16

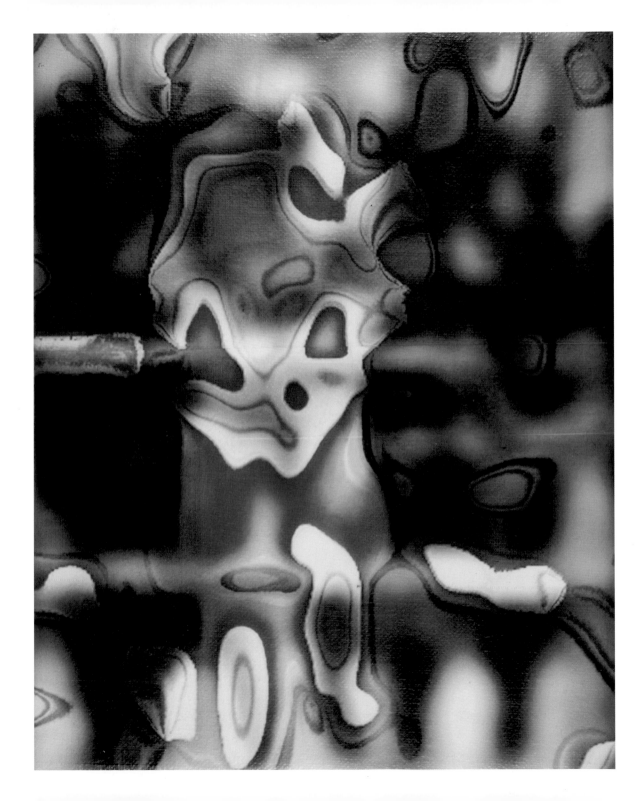

## List of works

1 **Guantanamerica** 2005
oil and acrylic on linen 46 x 78 in / 117 x 198 cm

2 **Submission I** 2005
oil on linen 34 x 36¼ in / 86.5 x 92 cm

3 **Submission II** 2005
oil on linen 34 x 36¼ in / 86.5 x 92 cm

4 **Submission III** 2006
oil on linen 34 x 36¼ in / 86.5 x 92 cm

5 **Submission IV** 2006
oil on linen  34 x 36¼ in / 86.5 x 92 cm

6 **Submission V** 2006
oil on linen 34 x 42¼ in / 86.5 x 107 cm

7 **Virus** 2006
inkjet transfer and acrylic on jute 56 x 51¼ in / 142.3 x 129.9 cm

8 **X-Ray** 2006
inkjet transfer and acrylic on linen 58 x 50 in / 147 x 127 cm

9 **Ink Blot Theory of Counter Terrorism** 2006
inkjet transfer and acrylic on jute 21¾ x 15¾ in / 55 x 40 cm

10 **Oil Interference Patterns #1** 2006
inkjet transfer and acrylic on jute  14 x 14 in / 35 x 35 cm

11 **Oil Interference Patterns # 2** 2006
inkjet transfer and acrylic on jute  14 x 14 in / 35 x 35 cm

12 **Oil Interference Patterns # 3** 2006
inkjet transfer and acrylic on jute  14 x 14 in / 35 x 35 cm

13 **Oil Interference Patterns # 4** 2006
inkjet transfer and acrylic on jute  14 x 14 in / 35 x 35 cm

14 **Oil Interference Patterns # 5** 2006
inkjet transfer and acrylic on jute  14 x 14 in / 35 x 35 cm

15 **Oil Interference Patterns # 6** 2006
inkjet transfer and acrylic on jute  14 x 14 in / 35 x 35 cm

16 **Oil Interference Patterns # 7** 2006
inkjet transfer and acrylic on jute  14 x 14 in / 35 x 35 cm

17 **Oil Interference Patterns # 8** 2006
inkjet transfer and acrylic on jute  17¾ x 14 in / 45 x 35 cm

## JOHN KEANE

| 1954 | Born Hertfordshire |
| 1972-76 | Camberwell School of Art |
| 2000- | Visiting Professor, The London Institute |
| 2000- | Visiting Research Fellow, Camberwell College of Arts |

## SOLO EXHIBITIONS

| 1980 | *Peking, Moscow, Milton Keynes*, Minsky's Gallery, London |
| 1982 | *Some of it* Works on Paper, Centre 181, London |
| 1984 | *War Efforts*, Pentonville Gallery, London |
| 1985 | *Conspiracy Theories*, Angela Flowers Gallery, London |
| | *Perspective 1985*, Basel Art Fair, Switzerland |
| 1986 | *Work Ethics*, Angela Flowers Gallery, London |
| 1988 | *Bee-Keeping in the War Zone*, Angela Flowers Gallery, London |
| | *Against the Wall*, Turnpike Gallery, Leigh, Greater Manchester |
| | *The Accident*, commissioned painting and screenprint for Greenpeace, Flowers East, London |
| 1989 | *Divided States*, Terry Dintenfass Gallery, New York |
| | Forum, Hamburg, Germany |
| 1990 | *The Other Cheek?*, Flowers East, London |
| 1991 | *Cloth Caps and Hang Gliding*, Angel Row Gallery, Nottingham |
| | *The Other Cheek?*, Arts Council Gallery, Belfast |
| | *Before The War*, Kelvingrove Art Gallery, Glasgow |
| 1992 | *Gulf*, Imperial War Museum, London; Northern Centre for Contemporary Art, Sunderland; Graves Art Gallery, Sheffield; Tullie House, Carlisle; Aberdeen Art Gallery, Aberdeen |
| | *Fairy Tales of London*, Lannon Cole Gallery, Chicago |
| | *Burden of Paradise*, Flowers East at London Fields, London |
| | *Not the Gulf*, Watermans Art Centre, London |
| 1993 | *The Struggle for Control of the Television Station*, Flowers East, London; Terry Dintenfass Gallery, New York |
| | *Gulf*, Norton Gallery, Palm Beach, Florida |
| 1994 | *The Struggle for Control of the Television Station*, |

Galerie Leuenberger, Zurich

*Five and a Half Years of Screenprints*, Flowers Graphics, London

*Fear of God*, Riverside Studios, London

| 1995 | *Works on Paper*, Flowers East at London Fields, London |
| | *Graham Greene and the Jungle of Human Dilemma*, Flowers East at London Fields, London |
| 1997 | *Truth, Lies & Super-8*, Flowers East at London Fields, London |
| | John Keane, Wellington College |
| | *John Keane A Painter in Focus*, Wolverhampton Art Gallery |
| | *Truth, Lies & Super-8: The Polyprints*, Riverside Studios, London |
| | *John Keane A Painter in Focus*, Ulster Museum, Belfast |
| | *Conflicts of Interest*, Laing Art Gallery, Newcastle-upon-Tyne |
| 1999 | *Trading Flaws and Sporting Mistakes*, Flowers West, Santa Monica |
| 2000 | *Prints and Monoprints*, Flowers Graphics |
| | *Making a Killing*, Flowers East at London Fields |
| | Gwenda Jay Addington Gallery, Chicago |
| 2001 | *Saving the Bloody Planet*, Flowers East, London |
| 2002 | *Saving the Bloody Planet*, Flowers West, Santa Monica |
| | *Recent Events*, Flowers Central, London |
| 2003 | *Events*, Galerie Behemot, Prague |
| 2004 | *The Inconvenience of History*, London Institute Gallery, London; The Naughton Gallery, Queen's University, Belfast; Greenbelt Festival; Derby Museum and Art Gallery; Aberystwyth Arts Centre |
| | *Back To Fundamentals*, Flowers East, London; Ferens Art Gallery, Kingston upon Hull |
| 2006 | *Fifty Seven Hours in the House of Culture*, Flowers East, London |
| | Andrei Sakharov Museum, Moscow |
| | *Guantanamerica*, Flowers, New York |

## SELECTED RESIDENCIES AND COMMISSIONS

| | |
|---|---|
| 1985-86 | Artist in Residence, Whitefield School, London |
| 1988 | Commissioned exhibition about Ollerton Mining Community, by Nottinghamshire County Council |
| 1991 | Official British War Artist, Gulf War |
| 1998 | Commissioned painting for The Lowry Centre Trust |
| 2000-01 | Artist in Residence, Independent on Sunday |
| 2000 | Project with Greenpeace UK in the Amazon rain forest |
| 2001 | Portrait of Mo Mowlam for the National Portrait gallery |
| 2002 | Project with Christian Aid in Israel and the Occupied Territories |
| 2005 | Portrait of Sir Bill Morris for the National Portrait Gallery |
| 2006 | Portrait of Greg Dyke for the BBC |
| | Project with Christian Aid in Angola |
| | Project with the Royal National Theatre, London to create an opera about the Moscow theatre siege |

## PUBLIC COLLECTIONS

Aberdeen Art Gallery
Arthur Anderson & Co.
Arts and Museum Section of Cleveland County Library and Leisure Department
British Coal
Chase Manhattan Bank, NA
Christie's Corporate Collection
Contemporary Art Society
Dain Rauscher Inc, USA
Detroit Institute of Fine Art, USA
Deutsche Bank
The Economist
The Financial Times
Glasgow Museums: Gallery of Modern Art
Harris Museum and Art Gallery, Preston
Hill Samuel Investment Services Group
Hull City Museums, Art Galleries and Archives
Leicestershire County Council
London Borough of Hammersmith and Fulham
The National Army Museum
National Portrait Gallery
National Power
Paintings in Hospitals
Rugby Museum
Trustees of the Imperial War Museum, London
Unilever
Ulster Museum
University College of Wales, Aberystwyth
Wolverhampton Museum and Art Gallery

John Keane, 2006

**Flowers**

1000 Madison Avenue
New York NY 10021
Tel:  +1 (212) 439 1700
Fax: +1 (212) 439 1525
newyork@flowerseast.com

**Flowers East / Flowers Graphics**

82 Kingsland Road
London E2 8DP
Tel:  + 44 (0) 20 7920 7777
Fax: + 44 (0) 20 7920 7770
gallery@flowerseast.com
graphics@flowerseast.com

**Flowers Central**

21 Cork Street
London W1S 3LZ
Tel:  + 44 (0) 20 7439 7766
Fax: + 44 (0) 20 7439 7733
central@flowerseast.com

**www.flowerseast.com**

rFlowers.

© John Keane
© Harold Pinter / Neal Katyal
Photography by Shaun McCracken
Designed by Peter Gladwin / Cover design John Keane
Printed by Specialblue
Coordinated by Cate Rickards

1000 copies

ISBN - 10 1 - 902945 - 84 - 0
ISBN - 13 978 - 1 - 902945 - 84 - 2